Blue Jenkins

Other Badger Biographies

Blue Jenkins

Working for Workers

Julia Pferdehirt

WISCONSIN HISTORICAL SOCIETY PRESS

Published by the Wisconsin Historical Society Press
Publishers since 1855

© 2011 by the State Historical Society of Wisconsin

For permission to reuse material from *Blue Jenkins: Working for Workers* (978-0-87020-427-2), please access www.copyright.com or contact the Copyright Clearance Center, Inc. (CCC), 222 Rosewood Drive, Danvers, MA 01923, 978-750-8400. CCC is a not-for-profit organization that provides licenses and registration for a variety of users.

wisconsin**history**.org

Photographs identified with WHi are from the Society's collections; address requests to reproduce these photos to the Visual Materials Archivist at Wisconsin Historical Society, 816 State Street, Madison, WI 53706.

Front and back cover photos: Courtesy of Betty Thomas

Printed in the United States of America
Cover and interior design by Jill Bremigan
Interior page composition by Biner Design

15 14 13 12 11   1 2 3 4 5

Library of Congress Cataloging-in-Publication Data

Pferdehirt, Julia, 1952–
  Blue Jenkins : working for workers / Julia Pferdehirt.
      p. cm.—(Badger biographies series)
  Includes bibliographical references and index.
  ISBN 978-0-87020-427-2 (pbk.)
1. Jenkins, William, 1916-1999. 2. African American labor leaders—Wisconsin—Racine—Biography.
3. Labor unions—Organizing—Wisconsin—Racine—History. 4. African Americans—Wisconsin—
Racine—Social conditions—20th century. 5. Racine (Wis.)—Race relations. 6. Racine (Wis.)—
Biography. I. Title.
  HD6509.J46P44 2011
  331.88092—dc23
  [B]
                                    2011022842

∞ The paper used in this publication meets the minimum requirements of the American National Standard for Information Sciences—Permanence of Paper for Printed Library Materials, ANSI Z39.48-1992.

On this day I am mindful of Blue Jenkins and a life dedicated
to protecting the rights of workers through unions where every
person has a voice. I dedicate this book to the teachers of the
state of Wisconsin. Every day you help shape the next generation.
It's impossible to thank you enough.

Publication was made possible, in part,
by the Alice E. Smith Fellowship.

Contents

1

Meet Blue Jenkins

On a few cold, wintry days in January of 1974, a historian from the Wisconsin Historical Society packed a tape recorder and notebooks into his car and traveled from Madison to Racine, Wisconsin, to meet William Jenkins. In his living room, William, called "Blue" by his friends and family, told a story that few people talked about in 1974. He told his own story. A story of growing up black in Wisconsin before the **Civil Rights Movement**.

Blue told the story of his life. He talked about moving from the South with his family when he was less than a year old. Blue's great-grandparents, and perhaps even his grandparents, lived in slavery. Blue's parents hoped for a better life in a big northern city.

Civil Rights Movement: the movement from the mid-1950s through the 1960s for African Americans to have fair and equal treatment under the law

Blue talked about what it was like to grow up in a neighborhood where everybody knew everybody—but blacks were still invisible. He talked about what it was like to grow up in a school where he excelled at sports—but couldn't always eat with the rest of the team when they traveled to games in other cities.

He talked about what it was like for his father—and later himself—to work in a **foundry** at a busy factory. He talked about joining a **labor union** and working for workers to be treated fairly in their workplaces no matter what color their skin was. He talked about becoming a leader in that union and giving workers a chance to be heard.

Blue Jenkins lived during years of great change. He lived through the **Great Depression** and three wars. He began working at a time when business owners could refuse to hire anyone black and nothing could be done about it.

Blue was part of the Civil Rights Movement. He knew what it was like to feel afraid of being hurt because he was

---

foundry (**foun** dree): a factory where metal is melted and shaped   **labor union** (**yoo** nyuhn): an organization of workers set up to improve things such as working conditions, health benefits, and the amount people are paid to work   **Great Depression**: the decade of the 1930s when many people in the United States had no jobs and were very poor

speaking about equality. He knew what it was like to have to fight for things to be fair.

Blue became a respected leader, not only in the black community but also in Wisconsin's labor unions. He worked to make unions accept black and white people equally.

Blue talked to the historian for more than 2 days. He filled tape after tape with stories of his life and experiences. He spoke about racism and friendship. About dancing to the music of the big bands and playing baseball every weekend. About fighting to get better jobs for black workers and about black and white workers **banding** together to get better jobs for everyone.

By sharing his life with us, Blue Jenkins gives us a way to understand what it was like to grow up black in Wisconsin 50, 60, or even 90 years ago. And he shows us how working for equality—in his community and in his workplace—is working for the good of people everywhere.

banding: forming a group to achieve a common purpose

2

Coming Up North

More than 90 years ago, good news came to Hattiesburg, Mississippi. Jobs! Factories and foundries in the North were looking for hard-working men.

Poor people in Mississippi, both black and white, worked long hours just to feed their families and have a place to live. In Hattiesburg, like much of the South, most land and businesses were owned by wealthy white men.

Many poor folks worked as coal miners. Others were **sharecroppers**. Sharecroppers didn't own farms. Instead, they rented their houses and fields from the landowners.

Every year sharecroppers would borrow money from the landowners. They bought seeds. They tilled and planted crops and worked from early in the morning to late in the evening.

sharecropper: a poor farmer who has no money to rent land to farm. To pay the rent, sharecroppers give the landowner a "share" of their crops.

4

These sharecroppers are picking cotton by hand.

This sharecropper's son is "worming" tobacco.

At harvest time, the first "share" of the crop went to the landowners. That "share" repaid the **seed money**—with **interest**, of course. The share paid rent for the house and land. After the landowner's share was paid, sharecroppers had very little left for food and clothes.

That was a sharecropper's life—they worked all year and, at the end, had no more than when they started. It was a life with no future. Some of Blue's family members were sharecroppers.

seed money: money borrowed to buy seeds or start a new business   **interest**: the cost for borrowing money, usually based on the amount borrowed

WHI IMAGE ID 11947

Coal mining was dangerous and dirty work.

As a young man, Blue's father was a coal miner. Coal mining was terrible, hard, dangerous work. Coal miners dug for coal in deep underground tunnels. Many mining companies refused to spend money to make the tunnels safe. Pay was very low. Miners died from cave-ins and got sick from breathing coal dust. While mining companies got rich, the miners' only future was more work, more coal dust, and more danger.

Some coal miners, like Blue's father, were part of a labor union. The union fought for better workplaces and **wages** for the workers who were part of the union. Still, change was very slow in coming. And for union members who were black, it was even harder. They faced **discrimination** on the job and in the union.

In 1916, the Jenkins family left Hattiesburg, Mississippi, in search of a new future. Frank Jenkins had tried many jobs to take care of his family. He worked for the railroads, **laying track**. He tried sharecropping and coal mining. Some of his relatives heard about jobs in Wisconsin, 900 miles north. Factories and foundries in the North needed workers. The Jenkins family wanted a better life. So Frank and his wife, Irene, packed up their belongings and headed to Wisconsin. They brought with them their 2 sons, Curtis, 4 years old, and William, only 6 months old.

---

wage: the money someone is paid to work   **discrimination**: unfair treatment of people, based on differences such as race, age, or place of birth   **laying track**: building train tracks

7

The Jenkins family came by train, riding through Chicago and north along the Lake Michigan shore to a town called **Racine** just south of Milwaukee. William's father had been offered a job at the J. I. Case foundry. But when he got there, plans changed. He found out he had been hired to take the place of a union worker. That union worker was **on strike** with his union to fight for better wages. Mr. Jenkins believed in

Main St. looking North from 5th St., Racine, Wis.

Downtown Racine in 1915

Racine: ruh **seen**   **on strike**: refusing to go to work until an employer agrees to change something

Blue's father
came to Racine
to work at the
J. I. Case foundry.

Blue's father worked
in a foundry, like these
men at Fairbanks,
Morse & Company.

unions. He had been part of a union, too, when he was a miner years before. He knew that if he took the job, it would hurt the union. So he turned the job down. Eventually, he would work in a foundry. Until then, he found a job building houses.

The family rented a house across from the train station. With fewer than 200 black people in the city, they soon knew everyone in the community. Their future had begun.

What Is a Labor Union?

Labor unions are **organized** groups of workers that try to improve their workplace. Labor unions have a long history in the United States and in Wisconsin. They have made jobs safer, fairer, and better paid.

Unions began because workers couldn't do much on their own to make their jobs better. Jobs were often dangerous and poorly paid. Sometimes bosses and factory owners didn't care about or listen to their workers. But if workers got together, they could organize labor unions. The unions then could make **demands** of employers, encouraging them to make workplaces better.

*Factory workers **assemble** parts for a tractor in a Chicago factory.*

organized: arranged in order to work together   **demand**: an official request   **assemble**: put together

10

This poster from 1916 shows ways to be safe while you work.

Most companies didn't like unions, and employers often made it hard for workers to join one. Sometimes employees would be fired for trying to start a union. Other times companies would try to stop workers by threatening them or giving them dangerous jobs.

Since the 1800s, unions have done a lot to improve workplaces. Once, people worked 12 hours a day or more. Unions fought for 8-hour days. Unions demanded safer work places. And they got workers better wages and **benefits**. Because of unions, workers in Wisconsin and around the world have better lives and better jobs.

benefit: a special advantage that comes with a job such as time off when you're sick

Little William grew into a friendly, **outgoing** boy. He ran everywhere, playing and meeting people. Somebody gave him a nickname. Soon, everyone in the neighborhood called him "Blue."

Sometimes Blue would run in through the front door of the house. "Mama," he'd shout, "I saw somebody today."

"Who?" his mother would ask.

Blue would smile. "Just somebody."

By "somebody" Blue meant somebody like me. Somebody black moving into our neighborhood.

Blue loved to race across the street and hang around the train station. He watched the trains roar by. He listened as the **brakeman** brought the huge machine grinding and hissing to a stop. **Conductors** took tickets and **porters** helped passengers with their baggage. It was a wonderful place for a curious, smart boy who was interested in everything and everyone.

outgoing: warm, friendly, and confident   **brakeman**: a train worker who operates the train's brakes
conductor: a train worker who collects tickets and keeps the train on schedule   **porter**: a train worker who handles luggage

Blue loved to greet newcomers at the Racine train depot.

And sometimes, somebody would step down from a train. Somebody black. Somebody coming to Racine to find a new future.

Maybe the person would smile at the small African American boy watching from the platform. The newcomer to Racine didn't know it, but he or she had just met Blue, the friendliest member of Racine's black community.

During Blue's childhood, many black men, women, and families arrived in Racine by train. Many came from the South looking for work just as Blue's family had. They were part of what is known as the "Great **Migration**," a time between 1916 and 1930 when many African Americans moved from the South to northern cities. The Great Migration began when factory owners needed workers to fill the jobs of men who had gone to fight in World War I.

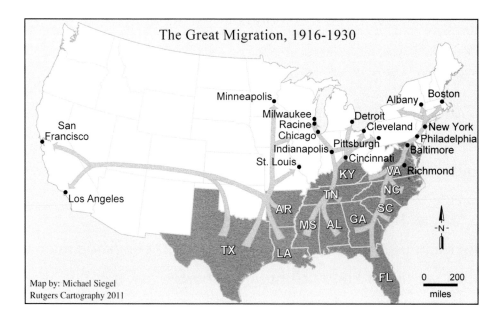

migration (mı **gray** shuhn): movement from one community to another in the same country

The owners knew that men from the South were willing to work very hard for low pay.

Frank and Irene Jenkins were generous and kind to newcomers. Blue remembered his mother inviting strangers to supper. He remembered whole families showing up at their door, tired and hungry after a long trip by train from the South.

Over time, Racine became known as a place for jobs. More and more men, black and white, came to work in the city, bringing their families and dreams of a new life.

What was it like to grow up in Blue's neighborhood?

In the 1920s, Racine was a hardworking factory town. People called it a "**blue collar**" town because factory and foundry workers wore blue shirts to work. "Blue collar" men worked with their hands. They did hard, physical labor. Only

blue collar: working with your hands instead of in an office or store

15

Blue-collar workers

White-collar workers

business owners and well-educated people wore starched and ironed white shirts to work. Those "**white collar**" jobs paid better. In the 1920s, most "white collar" workers were white.

Everyone in Racine's black community worked, men and women alike. Some people had "white collar" jobs like working at the post office. A few black people were teachers. But many more worked with their hands as **laborers**, **janitors**, or maids.

white collar: working at an office or store and not doing physical labor   **laborer**: someone who works with their hands doing physical labor   **janitor**: someone who takes care of and cleans a building

Women in the black community worked hard for little pay. They cleaned houses, washed clothes, and cooked for wealthy white people. Then they went home to clean their own houses and cook for their own families.

Some business owners only hired white men. They refused to hire any women or black people, no matter how honest, hardworking, or skilled they were. Why? It was just because of the color of their skin.

Today, many years later, Blue Jenkins's step-daughter, Betty Thomas, still tells the story of her mother's first job in Racine.

"My mother's family was one of the oldest, most respected black families in Racine. They'd lived in Wisconsin since the 1850s. When my mother was still in school she got a job at a local drug store at a **soda fountain**.

Soda fountains were popular gathering places.

soda fountain: a place where you can buy soda drinks, often with ice cream in them

17

Now, my mother was very **fair**—her skin was so light in color that people sometimes thought she was white. One day, a bunch of her friends came to visit from Chicago. They came to the drug store expecting to order something. The owner called my mother into the back room.

" 'Elouise,' he said, 'who are those people? Get them out of here. We don't serve **negroes** here and you know it.'

" 'Well,' Elouise said. 'You won't serve my friends, but you'll hire a negro?'

"The store owner shook his head. 'What do you mean, hire a negro?' he asked. Elouise looked him right in the eye. That was her way, she never stepped down. She told her boss that she was black. He was horrified. He even said, 'I won't tell if you don't. But, you've got to get those people out of the store.'

"Elouise's friends left. And so did she. She would rather lose a job than work for that man."

fair: having light-colored skin or hair   **negro**: a name people used in the past for African Americans. People now think the word is disrespectful.

African American Names

When Blue was young, black people were often called *negroes*. During slavery time, people from Africa were called *black*. Later, the names *negro* or *colored people* were used. Years passed. Some people thought it was disrespectful to call people "colored" or "negro." They began to use words like *Afro-Americans* or *African Americans*. Today, some people prefer the word *black*.

In the 1920s, about 50,000 people lived in Racine. Only about 250 people were African American. Many were unmarried. Some were families. About 20 black families lived in one neighborhood. There were moms, dads, grandparents, children, and grandchildren. Most of these people lived in the same neighborhood, about 4 or 5 square blocks.

The whole neighborhood watched out for each other. And Blue knew that if he played around or got into trouble, somebody would tap him on the shoulder and say, "Blue, you better go home now."

Like children growing up in the 1920s in communities all across the country, Blue Jenkins was raised and watched over by a family of families in a neighborhood where everyone knew everyone. And where everyone cared.

3
A New Life

Back in Mississippi, children from poor families, both black and white, usually went to school for just a few years. Some didn't go to school at all. Black and white children went to separate schools. Some people tried to say the schools were "**separate but equal**." They weren't.

A segregated school

separate but equal: the idea that blacks and whites could be made to use different restaurants, stores, schools, and other things, as long as the places and things were equally good

A girl named Ruby Bond came to Wisconsin from Pontotoc, Mississippi, around the same time Blue and his family came to Racine. She remembered that in Mississippi there were "colored schools." She remembered that white children went to a brick school. Black children went to a different school, an old one-room cabin with a leaky roof. The white children studied music and art. Black children didn't have special classes.

Mrs. Bond said the schools were separate and unequal. Unequal pay for teachers. Unequal money for books. Unequal everything.

In Mississippi, children from poor families rarely finished high school. When the family needed money, they would have to quit school to work. By the time girls were 15 or 16, they often got married and started families of their own.

Like many working people, Blue's parents had little education. His mother, Irene, had only gone to school until about third grade. His father couldn't read or write. As a boy, Frank didn't have the choice to go to school. He had to work in the mines to earn money for his family.

Mr. and Mrs. Jenkins brought their family to Racine for a better life. Education was one way to that future. By the time Blue was old enough to go to school, he and his older brother Curtis had 2 sisters, Dorothy and Mary. Blue and his sisters and brother all went to school. Their parents expected them to study hard and stay in school. Mr. and Mrs. Jenkins worked long hours so their children could get the education they never had.

In Racine in the 1920s and '30s, black and white children went to school together. In school, Blue was as friendly and outgoing as he'd always been. Soon, Blue was running and playing with Italian, Polish, German, Danish, and Latino boys.

"Separate but Equal"

After the **Civil War** ended in 1865, African Americans were free. But that didn't always mean they were equal. African Americans still faced discrimination. Often they couldn't live in the same places as white people, or work in the same jobs, shop in the same stores, or even use the same entrance to a building.

In the South, laws were written in the 1870s to keep black people separate from white people: separate schools, separate train cars, separate restaurants. These were called Jim Crow laws. Some people wanted black and white people to live separately because they believed white people were better than black people. Others believed all people were equal, but didn't believe blacks and whites should live together or be friends.

Too often, separate didn't mean equal. White schools were better than black schools.

In the South, black and white people were forced to use separate water fountains because of segregation.

Civil War: the war between the North and South of the United States, which took place between 1861 and 1865

White train cars were more comfortable than black train cars. White people sat at tables in restaurants while black people had to go to the back door and take their food home.

In Wisconsin in the 1930s, there weren't any Jim Crow laws. But African Americans were still kept separate in many ways. Blacks and whites lived in different neighborhoods, and white landlords wouldn't allow blacks to live anywhere else. Blacks also had trouble finding jobs. Many unions didn't allow black people to join, and so black workers couldn't get jobs where union membership was required. This was still discrimination.

WHI IMAGE ID 84375

Starting in the 1950s, African Americans began **protesting** *against discrimination as part of the Civil Rights Movement.*

The Civil Rights Movement of the 1950s and 1960s started to change much of this. Jim Crow laws stopped when the US government passed the Civil Rights Act and the Voting Rights Act.

Today, people no longer think separate is equal, but the fight to end discrimination continues, even in Wisconsin.

protesting: gathering in public to fight for a cause

When the black community of Racine was small, racial discrimination wasn't a big problem. But as more black people moved into town, some whites felt upset. These white people thought they had a right to be in charge of everything. They wanted to make sure black people didn't move into their neighborhoods or work in their businesses. Discrimination grew.

And as more black people moved to Racine, the black community itself began to change. At first, people came to Racine to make money in the foundries and factories. Money was like a magnet. It attracted people from Chicago and other cities. Soon, people came to Racine to make money in other ways.

Gamblers moved into the black community. Some people used their houses for wild parties and dances. When alcohol was outlawed during **Prohibition**, people called **bootleggers** sold it illegally. These newcomers were different from the miners and sharecroppers and their families who had come to Racine looking for a better future. They were tougher people.

gambler: someone who bets money on a game, race, or other contest   **Prohibition** (proh uh **bish** uhn): the period between 1920 and 1933 in which it was illegal to make or sell alcohol   **bootlegger**: someone who makes or sells alcohol illegally

Some people didn't like the gamblers and bootleggers. Black and white people worried that crime might increase. But one thing didn't change. The black community was still a place where people looked out for one another.

Blue went to school and worked hard. But when he wasn't in school, he could be found anywhere and everywhere in the community.

Years later, as an old man, Blue would laugh and remember his boyhood in Racine. He remembered hopping on the back of a streetcar or running around with friends. In summertime,

A ride on a streetcar cost 5 cents when Blue was a boy.

he'd scramble out of bed in the morning, grab something to eat, and be gone all day. He'd watch the older men play baseball. He'd watch the gamblers play dice and cards. He met black people and white people, **immigrants** and business owners. And everywhere he went, he made friends.

Blue and his friends didn't have much money, so they had to make their own fun. Blue could always gather his buddies for a game of ball or cards, or to catch fish in the river. Movies cost a nickel. Blue loved movies, even if black customers had to sit in the balcony while white people took the seats close to the screen.

A man walks the stairs to the black entrance of a movie theater.

immigrant (**im** uh gruhnt): someone who leaves a country to permanently live in another country

A 1930 Chevrolet

In 1928, Blue celebrated his twelfth birthday. His uncle brought a marvelous new object into the Jenkins family: a car! This uncle stayed in Racine for 6 months. When he left town, he gave the car to Blue's mother, Irene.

The car belonged to his mother, but Blue had plans for it! He learned that a new law had been passed requiring people to have a **license** to drive in Wisconsin. Before 1929, anyone could drive. Of course, not many people had cars. Traffic jams were as likely to involve horses and wagons as cars or trucks.

license: an official card that says a person is allowed to drive

How did someone get a driver's license? Blue asked around. Amazing! He learned that anyone could get a license just by mailing an **application** and about 2 dollars to a government office in Madison.

Blue got an application. The form asked for his name and address. The form didn't ask about his age. So Blue filled it out and sent in the 2 dollars. Then he waited. One day, an envelope arrived addressed to "Mr. William Jenkins." Blue ripped it open. There, signed, stamped, and officially approved, was a driver's license. He could drive!

It wasn't long before the law changed and drivers had to be 16 before they could get a license. But it was too late. Blue had his license. Although he was only 12 and wasn't tall enough to easily reach the brake and gas pedals, Blue was already driving his mother's car all over Racine!

application: a written request

4

On and Off the Ball Field

Blue Jenkins loved to play ball—any kind of game. When he was growing up, he and his friends needed nothing more than a baseball, a bat, and an empty lot to have fun. "Pick up" games of baseball and softball kept them happy on hot summer nights. Blue and his friends played everything—baseball in summer and football when school started each fall. They played basketball during the winter, and as soon as the snow melted they headed to the softball field.

LIBRARY OF CONGRESS LC-USZ62-96727

When Blue was in high school, he used sports **equipment** like this.

equipment: tools needed for a particular purpose

WILLIAM HORLICK HIGH SCHOOL

William Horlick High School

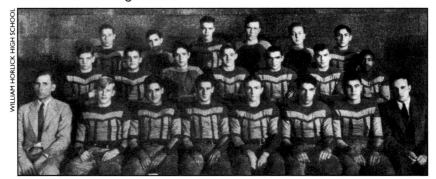

WILLIAM HORLICK HIGH SCHOOL

Blue is at the far right, second row, in this 1933 yearbook photo
of the Horlick High School football team.

Even before he got to high school, Blue made a name for
himself. He was allowed to play on the William Horlick High
School football team as an eighth grader. He was strong,
fast, and a good ball carrier. During his high school years, he
earned 4 **varsity letters** in football. By the time he was a senior,

varsity letter: a cloth letter given as an award to high school students for doing well in sports or other activities he said, "I did all—I'm not bragging—but I did all the kicking, passing, and most of the running. I made all-state in football."

He loved playing. He also loved traveling to other cities and towns to play.

On those trips, the players talked, laughed, told stories, and played jokes on each other. They'd pile into a couple of cars and head for Beloit or Madison, Kenosha or Milwaukee to play against other teams. After a game, the coach would take the whole team to a restaurant for supper. And those guys loved to eat as much as they loved to play ball. Imagine the plates piled high with spaghetti or burgers and fries!

These trips took Blue to small towns and big cities. He met new people of all kinds. The football trips also brought Blue face-to-face with racism and discrimination. Horlick High School's teams were **integrated**. Black and white players

integrated: made to include people of all races

practiced, played, rode to games, and hung out together. But not all schools were like Horlick High. Some towns had no black citizens—not even one. In other cities, like Madison and Milwaukee, some schools were integrated and some had only white students.

In Racine, Blue had experienced racism. He had experienced violence and fear. Once, a hate-group called the **Ku Klux Klan** had gathered outside Blue's house. Blue's father was a leader in the black community, so the Klan wanted to frighten him. They hung a cloth figure made to look like a

person from the tree in front of the Jenkins's house. The figure was a way of saying, *Keep in your place, or this could be you.*

The Ku Klux Klan in Racine

Ku Klux Klan: a racist group that believes whites are better than other races

Blue was terrified. His dad sat in the living room with a shotgun, hoping he wouldn't have to use it to defend his family. Blue never forgot this.

Blue had also experienced hidden, quiet racism. He knew which restaurants and businesses in Racine wouldn't serve black customers. He just stayed away from those places. "No sense making trouble for anybody," he'd say.

People in the black community feared they would lose their jobs or be beaten up if they refused to act the way white people wanted them to act. People called this "staying in your place."

Blue had felt the hurt of discrimination. He knew what it was like to feel frightened and unsafe. He knew what it was like to be silent when he really wanted to say, *I deserve to be treated the same as anyone else*.

When football practice started each August, Coach Taylor would post the schedule for the season's games. Every year,

Blue's school played in Wisconsin cities where no black people lived. In some of these cities, Horlick High's black players weren't welcome. Every year, Blue's team played against these schools. And every year, Blue felt anger, embarrassment, and frustration.

In many towns, restaurant owners didn't want black customers. But they didn't dare turn the entire team away. In other towns, Blue and other black players experienced discrimination that Blue never forgot.

Blue said, "I'd go to Beloit and I'd be scared to go anyplace. We played Beloit one year, and they wouldn't let me eat in a restaurant there. I was the only black on the team."

Blue was good on the football field and the basketball court. Players from other teams learned to watch out for the strong, fast player from Racine. The Racine players respected him too. That's why, as Blue began his senior year in high school, the players chose him as captain of the football team.

In the 1930s, just like today, many young men dream of being chosen captain of their school's football team. But for Blue, such a dream seemed impossible. No black player had ever been chosen captain.

This cartoon was printed in Blue's high school yearbook. What did Blue dream of?

What an honor! But that honor was almost stolen by racism. Even when he was a grown man, Blue remembered every detail.

"I respect Coach Taylor so much," Blue said. "When I was going to high school, I was elected football captain in my last year. [We had a] banquet that night and the next day, I came to school, and the coach called me down to his office.

"Coach said, 'Hey, you been hearing any **rumors**?'

"I said, 'No.' I didn't know what he was talking about.

rumor: talk or an opinion that people tell each other, passing it on without knowing if it is true or not

"Coach said, 'A [bunch] of white people, parents, came up to school the other day, and they said they didn't want you to be captain of the football team. Just because you're black . . . they didn't want you to be over white kids.'

"Now I was looking for one thing," Blue said. "I only wanted one thing out of high school. I wanted to be the best. I said, 'Well, it doesn't make any difference to me, Coach, as long as I play.'

"Now, Coach was a big guy, about six feet three or four and weighed about two [hundred] twenty [pounds]. I was small. He grabbed me, and he picked me up! He said, 'Blue, I've been knowing you practically all your life. And you mean to tell me you're going to back down because these people said that? You stand up and fight.'

"Coach said, 'You can't go through life taking that from people just because you're a Negro.'

"But, I wanted to play!

"Coach said, 'I told them if you weren't captain, I wouldn't be coach.'

"That shook me up pretty good. I said, 'Well, how did you come out?'

"The coach smiled and said, 'Well, I'm going to coach.'

"He took a stand with those people," Blue said. "That was beautiful. It was wonderful … And that was in the 1930s!"

Coach Taylor had the courage to do right regardless of what anyone else said or did. To stand up to a crowd of white parents took courage. The fact that it happened about 80 years ago, when discrimination was considered normal by most people, is even more **remarkable**.

remarkable: worth noticing

5

Dreams Cut Short

It was 1935. In a few months, Blue was going to graduate from Horlick High School. He was the first member of his family ever to graduate. But Blue dreamed of more. He dreamed of going to college.

WILLIAM HORLICK HIGH SCHOOL

By the time he was a senior, Blue was the star of the football team.

Many of Blue's friends, both white and black, never finished high school. When foundries or factories offered good wages and quick money could be made gambling, many young men **dropped out**.

Blue said most of his black friends "went *to* high school, but not through. Most of them dropped out. [Some] went to

dropped out: quit going to school

40

vocational school. Only about 6 of us went to high school and finished."

Blue said, "These were smart kids. [All] of them were. But we never had an *image* here in Racine. What was our image? Going to work in the foundry. Working hard. Shining shoes, washing windows downtown, sweeping floors in an office building."

That "image" of life for black people in Racine **affected** the way many of Blue's friends thought and acted. They looked around at the adults in the black community. They saw hardworking people and loving

Many people in Racine saw African American men as foundry workers and railroad porters.

vocational school: a school where students learn specific skills that help them get jobs as laborers
affected: changed or influenced

families. They saw respected leaders working in the post office or in **maintenance** or at the foundry.

Blue and his friends knew black foundry workers did difficult jobs. The foundries couldn't run without them. Many black workers were experienced and skilled enough to be bosses in the foundries or **managers** in business. But because they were African American, racism and discrimination meant the doors to those jobs were closed to them.

Blue and his friends also noticed that few black adults owned businesses. The first black doctor didn't come to Racine until the 1960s, nearly 30 years after Blue finished high school. Many businesses discriminated against black people. Most young men and women didn't think they could go to college. They didn't see themselves as bank presidents or bosses. They accepted the "image" that black people in Racine could only work with their hands.

Blue dreamed of bigger things. He hoped his skill on the football field or the basketball court might lead to a college

maintenance (**mayn** tuh nuhns): fixing or maintaining machines or buildings **manager**: a person in charge of a business or other employees at work

Blue was the only black player on Horlick's 1936 football team.

scholarship. Still, the "image" and the racism behind it had an effect on Blue.

Blue told what happened. "My father had died. One of my coaches, **Leigh** Steinman, was going to get me a scholarship at Ripon College. It was for football."

Blue's scholarship would have paid for **tuition** and books. The school offered Blue a job working in the cafeteria that paid 15 dollars a month.

Blue felt uncertain and confused. With his father gone, his family couldn't help him pay for college. The scholarship

---

scholarship (**skah** ler ship): money given to help a student continue studying   **Leigh:** lee   **tuition:** money paid to take classes

MAP BY JOEL HEIMAN

Ripon

Racine

and his job would give him enough money for food. But he wasn't sure it would be enough to pay for a place to live. He'd have to leave his family and live miles away.

Then Coach Steinman called him into his office. Blue remembered, "Coach told me about the scholarship and then he said, 'You know, Jenkins, there's never been a Negro at Ripon. You know, when you go up there, you're going to have to stay in your place.'"

Blue felt like he'd been hit in the stomach. All his doubts about leaving home grew bigger and more confusing.

UNIVERSITY OF WISCONSIN ARCHIVES

The University of Wisconsin varsity squad in 1930. How many black players do you see?

44

"Boy, that hit me like a ton of bricks," Blue said. "Coach had never known me to do anything to upset anybody. In fact, I didn't do any socializing with white students because I knew how people were. I stayed in my place."

Blue realized he would be the only African American student at Ripon College. He might be the only black person in the entire town! He must have remembered how it felt to be the only black player on Horlick High's basketball team. Maybe he remembered those football trips to cities where he wasn't allowed to eat in restaurants. Maybe he thought about making friends and dating girls. Suddenly, he felt very alone. Perhaps he even felt afraid.

Blue had doubts about going to college because he wasn't sure he had enough money. He worried about how his mother and family would get along if he didn't work and contribute money. But his coach's words really did make Blue think hard about his dream of going to college. He said no to Ripon's scholarship. Blue decided to stay in Racine and get a job.

6

Working Hard and Playing Hard

In January of 1936, Blue graduated from high school and went out looking for work. But jobs weren't easy to find. When Blue was a boy, business was booming. Foundries and factories had so much work they couldn't find enough workers to do it all. But during the Great Depression, things changed in Racine and across the whole United States.

Blue was in high school during the Depression. Across the whole country, business was bad. Many people were out of work. By the time Blue graduated, things were just starting to get better.

Blue was a hard worker. He worked in a foundry until he was **laid off**. Being laid off meant workers lost their jobs because the business didn't have enough customers or buyers for their products. After that, Blue worked in a **junkyard**.

laid off: let go from a job because there isn't enough work to do or enough money to pay workers
junkyard: a place that collects and resells old stuff no one wants, such as wrecked cars

It was hard labor, but he was happy to have a paying job.

Blue moved from job to job. At one point, he worked in Chicago. When he returned to Racine, he was the talk of the whole black community. Blue came back wearing a fancy **zoot suit** and acting like a big-city Chicago boy.

And in 1938, he landed a job that he would have for 30 years: at Belle City **Malleable**, one of Racine's foundries.

Zoot suits became popular in the 1940s.

Although Blue worked hard, he also played hard. He was young, **single**, and fun-loving. He had money in his pocket and a love for living. He loved sports, pretty girls, and dancing.

---

zoot suit: a special suit with a long jacket, big shoulders, and baggy pants   **malleable** (**mal** ee uh buhl): soft and easy to shape   **single**: not married

47

Duke Ellington was a famous jazz composer and band leader.

WILLIAM P. GOTTLIEB/IRA AND LEONORE S. GERSHWIN FUND COLLECTION, MUSIC DIVISION, LIBRARY OF CONGRESS

"Milwaukee used to be one of the biggest areas for big bands to come in," Blue said. "All the big bands—Duke Ellington, Woody Herman—used to come to the Riverside Theatre. It had good music and the finest dancers."

Blue and his friends liked **swing dancing**. Swing-dance music was played on the radio, record player, or **live** by big bands with 15, 20, or even 30 musicians. Musicians played "rhythm" instruments like pianos, bass, and drums and "melody" instruments like clarinet, trumpet, saxophone, and guitar. The music was jazzy and fast. Dancers swung each other around. Sometimes the boy lifted the girl above his head.

swing dancing: energetic dancing done to band music that was popular in the 1930s   **live**: in person at a concert, not recorded

Jazz and swing dancing started in black communities like New Orleans in the South and New York City and Chicago in the North. In those cities and other places, black folks went to "**social clubs**" to dance and have fun. Sometimes, Blue and his friends would drive all the way to Milwaukee and dance the night away. In summer, they might drive out to Lake Ivanhoe, where a few wealthy black families built big houses and had a dance **pavilion**.

But they didn't always have to go so far to have fun. "We had social clubs right here in Racine," Blue remembered.

WHI IMAGE ID 50463

The Jitterbug was a popular dance style when Blue was a young man.

social club: a place similar to a restaurant or a bar where people meet to have fun   **pavilion**: a building with open sides used for outdoor music and dancing

"A really good club called the Hi-Lites was about the **swingingest** club between Minneapolis and Chicago. Once a year they'd give a big bash and invite the whole black community. It was called June Night."

The Hi-Lites parties were fancy. Women wore long dresses. Men wore formal black coats, a white shirt, and a black tie. "We'd *fall out*," Blue said. That meant everybody dressed in their finest, fanciest clothes and danced until the band was worn out and the food was gone.

When Blue wasn't working or dancing, he played and watched baseball or softball. Blue played sports at a time when some **professional sports** teams only hired white

In 1924, the first "Colored World Series" was held in Kansas City, Missouri.

swingingest: a slang word for most fun or exciting   **professional sports**: sports played at a high level and where the players are paid to play

players. Other teams were "separate but unequal." Baseball was played in 2 separate leagues, the Major League for white players and a separate Negro League for black players.

"We had a fellow called Chalky Jackson," Blue remembered. "Chalky, had he been white, would have been in the **big time** as an **ace** pitcher. But he played on the old Racine black baseball team, the Colored Athletics."

Blue remembered a catcher named Willus Westmoreland. "He was a wonder boy behind the plate," Blue said. Willus wore a **chest protector** with "Thou Shalt not Steal" written on it. "He could really throw," Blue said. "If he'd been white, I know he'd have been in the big leagues."

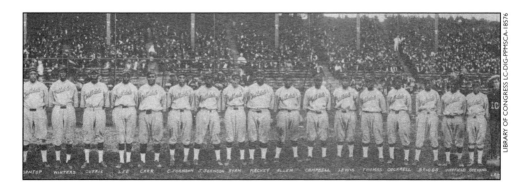

big time: the top level, as in the Major League   **ace:** very good   **chest protector**: a pad worn to shield a catcher's chest

51

If they were good enough, white players could try out for a Major League team where the money was good and the stadiums were packed. The best that black players could hope for was a spot on a team in the Negro League. Pay in the Negro League was very low. Negro League teams weren't welcome in the big, fancy stadiums. But games in the Negro League were fierce and the players were fiery.

Blue's friend Willus Westmoreland never made it to the "big leagues." He broke a law and went to prison. In the Negro League, he barely made enough money to pay for rent and food. Blue wondered if Westmoreland would have ended up in prison if he had been allowed to play in the major leagues.

Negro League Baseball

When baseball became popular in the late 1800s, everybody wanted to play. It seemed like the whole country had gone crazy for baseball. People made teams with their friends or coworkers. Kids played in whatever open field they could find. Some baseball teams even travelled around and challenged other teams, just for the fun of it.

Soon teams could charge money for people to watch them play. This was the beginning of professional baseball.

Early on, a few African Americans played on professional teams. Moses Fleetwood Walker and his brother, Welday Wilberforce Walker, played in the major leagues in the 1880s. But in 1888, the major leagues decided not to let blacks play on their teams any more.

But the Walkers and others still wanted to play ball! All-black leagues were started. There were many leagues, some only lasting a season or less. The ones the lasted for a while became known as Negro League Baseball.

The Negro League was most popular during and after the 1920s and 1930s. In August 1944, the East-West All-Star Game between the best players from the Negro National League

LIBRARY OF CONGRESS LC-DIG-PPMSC-00039

Jackie Robinson was the first black player in the Major Leagues. Before that, he was on a Negro League Team, the KC Monarchs.

and the Negro American League was played in front of 46,000 fans at **Comiskey** Park in Chicago. This was a bigger crowd than came to any Major League Baseball game on that day!

Players in the Negro League were just as good as the players in the major league, sometimes even better. Players like Satchel Paige, Cool Papa Bell, and Josh Gibson were eventually honored in the Baseball Hall of Fame.

In 1946, Jackie Robinson **signed on** with the Brooklyn Dodgers of Major League Baseball. He became the first black player to begin the integration of the major league. With integration came the end of "separate but unequal" sports teams. It also meant the end of the Negro League. Black players no longer had to play on separate teams.

Blue was a good ball player, but he wasn't good enough to try out for the Negro League. Instead, Blue and other young men formed their own **semi-professional** baseball league. Weekend after weekend, Blue and his buddies piled into cars and drove to other cities and states to play baseball. Businesses often **sponsored** semi-pro teams of white players.

Comiskey: koh **mis** kee   **signed on**: agreed to work for   **semi-professional**: playing for money, but not all the time   **sponsored**: gave money and support to, usually in return for some advertising

But few black teams found sponsors. The black players had to buy their own uniforms and set up their own schedules playing other black teams.

Blue's semi-pro team traveled around Wisconsin and Illinois. Sometimes they'd pass the hat after the game to get gas money for the drive back home. Sometimes they'd play for $50 and supper. Mostly, they just had fun.

7

Hard Times and Changes

It was 1941. Blue was 25 years old and working at Belle City Malleable in Racine. At the foundry, all the bosses were white. **Skilled jobs** were held mostly by white men. But things were about to change.

An African American factory worker and two white bosses

Across the ocean in Europe, World War II had started. A man named Adolph Hitler was **chancellor** of Germany. He wanted Germany to take over Europe. He wanted to **conquer** every other country and kill any person who wasn't white, strong, and smart. To carry out Hitler's plans, the German army invaded country

skilled job: a job that requires special training and usually pays well   **chancellor** (**chan** suh lur): the leader of a country, similar to a president   **conquer** (**kong** kur): beat and become master of

56

after country. Some countries fought back. Some countries became Germany's partners or **allies**.

The United States was worried about what was happening in Europe but didn't want to get involved. America waited and watched. Then, on December 7, 1941, Japan, one of Germany's allies, sent airplanes to bomb American ships in Pearl Harbor, Hawaii. It was a surprise attack. Many sailors were killed. Americans were **outraged**. The next day, our country declared war on Japan. A few days later, Germany declared war on the United States.

The attack on Pearl Harbor in 1941

WHI IMAGE ID 36604

ally (al I): friend, especially during a war   **outraged**: very angry

57

Suddenly, thousands of men joined the army to fight against Germany and its allies. Blue and his friends were as upset and angry about the bombing at Pearl Harbor as any American. African Americans across the United Sates wanted to defend their country, but because of racism and discrimination, most black volunteers were turned away.

Black men had been soldiers in every war ever fought by the United States. But as World War II began, the whole US Army had only 4 **units** of black soldiers and only 5 black officers. In the Navy, black sailors were only allowed to do laundry and shine shoes for officers, work as cooks or dishwashers, or load cargo on ships. No black men were allowed in the Marines.

NATIONAL ARCHIVES 80-G-469560

These men are "steward's mates," members of the Navy who set the table and cleaned up after meals.

unit: a military group of small size

Thousands and thousands of white men joined the military. They left jobs and families. Suddenly, factories, businesses, and shops needed thousands of workers.

Imagine. Black men were turned away from the military because of racism. Business owners were desperate for workers. The same men who were turned away from the military applied for the jobs left by white workers. Foundries and factories needed workers. They also needed experienced bosses to fill jobs left by white soldiers.

Soon, skilled black men who would never have been hired as bosses were being hired. Black men who had worked as laborers for years were **promoted**.

America wasn't prepared for war. Black workers played an important part in getting our country ready to fight. Trucks, tanks, ships, and submarines had to be built. Guns and equipment had to be made and shipped to US troops around the world. In Racine, J. I. Case turned its whole factory over

promoted: moved to a higher rank or job

to making airplane wings. A company called **Massey-Harris** made tanks. Other companies made parts for trucks, guns, and **shells**.

Three African American men assemble a cockpit in a factory during World War II.

As the war continued, the number of black workers in American business grew. Just as they had when Blue was a boy, more black workers left the South to find jobs in the North. In cities like Racine, Milwaukee, and Chicago, black workers were **recruited** to work in factories.

Women—both black and white—were also able to work in factories for the war effort. Even though the war was difficult for everyone, it allowed **minorities** and women to have good jobs.

Massey-Harris: **mas** ee **hair** uhs encouraged to work for a company larger race or ethnic group

shell: a small bomb that is fired from a cannon or tank **recruited**: **minority**: someone of a small race or ethnic group that lives among a

When the war began, Blue was working as a **swing grinder** at Belle City. His job took tremendous strength. He guided a big grinding machine to smooth rough spots on **cast-iron** machine parts. During the war, he became more than a swing grinder. He became a leader in the union.

Two laws helped to change the way unions worked during this time. In 1935, the US government passed the National Labor Relations Act, which gave unions the right to organize. The unions also got **collective bargaining rights**. This meant that employers had to sit down with union members and have both sides agree to what was fair.

And in 1941, President Roosevelt created the Fair Employment Practices **Committee**. Its job was to make sure that the factories that made war equipment did not discriminate against their workers. They had to be fair when they hired a new worker, and they had to be fair to those who already had jobs. Now people of any race or religion could work in these factories.

swing grinder: a worker who uses a grinding machine that hangs from a chain   **cast iron**: iron mixed with other metals to form a very hard metal   **collective bargaining rights**: the right of employees to come to an agreement with their employer about wages, hours, and other things   **committee** (kuh **mit** ee): a group of people chosen to go over a topic and make a decision

WHI IMAGE ID 2946

Members of the UAW in 1946. They are in line to vote for union leaders.

Blue was member of the United Auto Workers Union, or UAW, which had organized in 1935. The UAW was a union for people who worked in the **automotive industry**. Belle City made parts for cars before the war. Now it made parts for airplanes.

The UAW was one of the first unions that allowed African Americans to join. Even before the war began, Blue started to take part in the UAW. In 1940, Blue and some other union

automotive industry: the companies that make cars and other vehicles

men began to work for fair treatment for all workers. Blue couldn't have dreamed how important that work would become when the war ended.

World War II lasted 4 years. As time passed, more black men were allowed to enlist as soldiers, sailors, and Marines. More white men enlisted too. Some Wisconsin foundries recruited black workers from nearby countries like Jamaica, Haiti, Barbados, and the Dominican Republic to replace these workers.

NATIONAL ARCHIVES 44-PA-1217

The man on this poster is a Tusgekee Airman, a black pilot trained during World War II.

Even though the Fair Employment law was in place, new black workers were not treated well. They were paid less than white men had been paid to do the same jobs. Housing was a problem too. In Racine, the foundry owners built **shabby**, poorly heated buildings and bought trailers where new black workers were expected to live. The buildings and trailers were crowded. People were crammed together. Sometimes 2 men would share a bed. One man worked in the day and slept at night. The other man worked the night shift and slept in the day!

Black workers needed to eat. So Blue's mother and aunt opened a restaurant called the Chicken Shack. They knew just what working men wanted—good food and lots of it. When the foundries gave turkeys to workers for Thanksgiving or Christmas, the men would line up outside the Chicken Shack. They paid Irene Jenkins to bake their turkeys for them.

During the war, Blue became more involved in the union. He soon realized black workers needed the union. At a Fair Employment meeting in Milwaukee, he met some men from the UAW in Detroit. In Detroit, there had been a lot of discrimination in the unions. These men had been fighting against discrimination since the 1930s.

shabby: dirty and poorly made

64

FEPC stands for Fair Employment Practices Committee. This poster
called for fair hiring of blacks and whites.

Blue said, "I talked to these guys and got their views on the
way blacks were treated in other places than Racine, because
we were never treated the same way here." Discrimination
wasn't as bad in Racine as it was in other places. But that
didn't mean it didn't exist.

Blue said, "It makes it a little different to get started in a place where you're treated halfway right." He urged his friends to pay the **dues** and join the union.

Blue was looking ahead. He realized that when the war ended, the white workers would return and get their jobs back. Blue was smart. He knew that joining the union would be the only chance new black workers would have to keep their jobs once the white workers returned. Once the war was over, the Fair Practices law would stop.

Then, in 1945, the war ended. Blue was right: white workers came home. Of course, it was only fair that they would get their old jobs back. After all, they had left to defend America. But what would happen to all the black workers who had left their homes to work in Racine? Blue explained in his own words:

"What made me get active in the union was when, during the war, they recruited a lot of blacks from the South and from Jamaica and Barbados. They misused these guys. What

dues: money paid to an organization, such as a union, to help it run

WHI IMAGE ID 41243

These UAW members went on strike in West Allis in 1946. What does their **picket sign** say?

did they know about union **contracts**? They were really discriminated against. It was bad.

"And then, when the war was over, what really put the icing on the cake was that the whites wanted the blacks out. They knew they couldn't make the southerners go back south, but they could get the Jamaicans and Barbadians out of there and send them back to their countries.

picket sign: a sign carried by a protester during a strike   **contract**: an agreement between a worker and an employer about pay and other issues

67

"Some guys got up in the union meeting and said, 'Send [them] back in **cattle cars** if you have to.'

"There were only 3 blacks at the meeting that day. I said, 'Did you hear that guy?' Then I **blew my top**. I got pretty excited at that meeting."

Blue fought for the men from the South. He argued that the union had to stand up for every worker, even the men from other countries. Blue knew the men from Jamaica

In 1945, African Americans marched for equal rights in Milwaukee. The sign on the truck says, "We Helped **Lick** Hitler, Now We Want Decent Jobs and Homes!"

cattle cars: trailers used for shipping animals from one place to another   **blew my top**: got really angry
lick: beat

and Barbados would lose their jobs. But he demanded that they be fairly treated like any other laid off worker. If they were going to be laid off, they should receive some pay. Blue remembered, "The blacks started coming to me when they heard about what I did at the meeting. Then, when the whites saw the blacks coming to me, they started coming too. So up pops a black leader, which was me."

Nellie Wilson:
A Black Woman in the Union

It wasn't only black men who got hired during World War II. Companies also hired women to fill jobs.

In 1940, Nellie Wilson was a young black woman trying to feed her children. But she was having trouble. "Of all the places I went, I never once got a **job interview**," she said. But white women had no trouble when they applied for the same jobs.

Nellie heard there were good jobs at A.O. Smith, a Milwaukee company that made steel products. During World War II, A.O. Smith built **bombers** for the US Army. Nellie got a job

job interview: a meeting to see if someone should be hired for a job   **bomber**: a plane whose main job is to drop bombs on targets

69

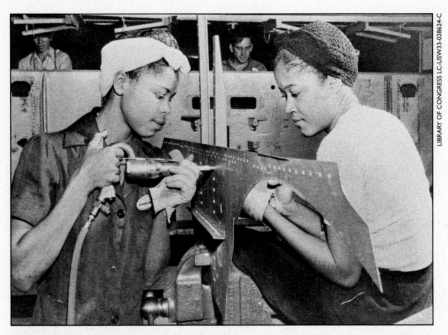

LIBRARY OF CONGRESS LC-USW33-028624-C

Black women had more job opportunities because of the war. These women worked at a factory that made airplanes.

measuring airplane **propellers**. "Best job I ever had in my life," Nellie said.

The workers at A. O. Smith had a union, and the union looked out for all workers—blacks and women too. When soldiers came back from the war and needed jobs, many companies fired their black and women workers to make room. But the union said no!

propellers: spinning blades that move an airplane through the air or a boat through the water

70

This surprised Nellie. "I couldn't believe it. It was simply incredible." They were "telling me about brotherhood, equality, and **fraternity** after I had suffered a lifetime of discrimination." The union treated the women and African Americans equally and made sure their jobs were just as safe as those of other workers. The union also tried to make sure women got the same amount of pay as men for the same work.

Nellie appreciated what the union did, so she got involved. When the union needed a new **steward** to make sure rules were followed, they asked Nellie if she would do it. She eventually became the first black woman elected to an **office** in her union. She worked for many years to make sure union workers were treated fairly. Nellie said, "The union has enabled me and mine to live comfortable lives, and it provided me with a lifetime of challenges."

Nellie Wilson in 1989

fraternity: a feeling of equality among people   **steward** (**stoo** urd): a union member who works with the company to make sure both the company and the union are following their contract   **office**: a leadership job

71

8

A Sit-Down Strike

During the war, Blue's union had worked to get **vacation pay** for workers. Until that time, if workers went on vacation or even took time off for a wedding or funeral, they weren't paid. Some people worked year after year without a single vacation because they couldn't afford not to be paid.

When the war ended and white workers returned to their jobs, the foundry owners saw their chance to take back workers' vacation pay. The workers and owners had signed a contract. The contract was good for

A man signs a union contract.

vacation pay: pay for workers on days they don't come in to work but instead go on vacation

one year and said exactly what both sides agreed to. When the year was over, the owners wanted to change the contract and take out vacation pay.

The owners had a plan. First, they would take vacation pay out of the contract. Then they would try to "break" other parts of the contract so they could pay lower wages or make workers work more hours. The owners hoped black and white union members wouldn't stand together. They wanted to divide the workers and take advantage of them.

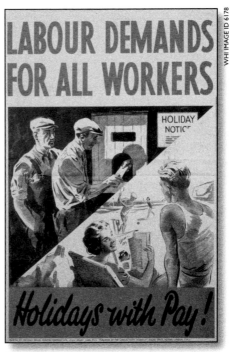

This poster made union members think about vacation or "holiday" pay.

Soon every union worker in the foundry was talking about vacation pay. Blue and other union leaders gathered to plan. What could they do to show the owners that black and white workers would stand together?

It started with Blue. He sat down in front of the huge grinding machine where he worked. When the boss came over, Blue said he just didn't feel like working.

Soon other workers sat down. The bosses knew this was called a "**sit-down strike**." The men didn't go home. They didn't march in front of the factory with signs. They just wouldn't do any work.

This was a dangerous, risky thing to do, and Blue knew it. But he did it anyway. He knew the workers had to stick together and not give up.

Unions had ways to make owners listen to their demands. Workers in other cities had held sit-down strikes, carried picket signs, and organized protest marches to stop owners from breaking contracts. Sometimes workers were fired. Sometimes owners responded with violence.

When union workers went on strike, some owners just fired the striking workers and hired new men. Union members called the new workers "**scabs**." No union member,

sit-down strike: a strike where workers refuse to work and just sit down on the job instead   **scab**: a worker who takes the job of someone on strike

In 1946, city workers in Milwaukee marched outside city hall to demand better pay.

or even their family and friends, would work as a scab. Just like Blue's father refused to take the job of a union worker when he moved to Racine, union men wouldn't take jobs at a factory during a strike. For a union man, having no job was better than working as a scab.

Other owners hired tough men called "thugs" to beat up workers who dared to go on strike. In Detroit, owners got the police to arrest striking workers. In the South, coal miners were actually killed because they went on strike to demand safer working conditions and better pay.

Blue wasn't worried about being beaten up. But he was nervous that the owners would find scabs to replace union workers. And Blue knew that if the owners were able to break one agreement, they would break others. Then the workers' contract would be worthless. Blue was determined to protect the rights of workers for fair treatment, decent pay, and safe working conditions.

So Blue sat down on the foundry floor. Here's the story in his own words:

"I got about 15, 20 guys in my department to sit down. And so, when the boss saw it, I said, 'Until the owners make up their mind what they're going to do, I'm gonna sit down here.'"

The bosses found a white worker named Murphy who was afraid. Murphy told the bosses, "Guys will go back to work if

Blue will go back to work." Blue was the only black worker in his department, and Murphy tried to blame the whole sit-down strike on him.

The bosses came to Blue. "You bring Murphy here," Blue demanded. When Murphy had to look Blue in the eye, he told the truth: he'd been talking to the company owners. The men in the department were on the side of the union. They sat down with Blue. And soon men in other departments sat down too.

"We won that part of the contract," Blue said. "When they found out we had sat down in the steel shop, the men in the **core room** sat down. That shut the whole foundry down!" Then Blue began to laugh. He said, "They thought I was the **instigator** of the whole thing . . . which I was, you know!"

---

core room: a room of a foundry where the molds used to shape metal are made   **instigator** (**in** stuh gay tur): the person who starts something

9

Moving Up in the Union

Between 1938 and 1968, Blue Jenkins worked in one Racine foundry, Belle City Malleable. That's 30 years! Every day he went to work and he worked hard.

"I've held practically every job in the foundry," Blue said. "I've been a molder, form pourer, ladle man, charge man, swing grinder, air grinder, air chipper, stand grinder, shake-out man, iron pourer, and, at times, inspector."

Foundry workers making molds of wheel parts

One of Blue's jobs was as a foundry ladle man. In this job, workers carried metal thousands of degrees hot!

In 1950, Blue married the love of his life, **Elouise** Bray. She came from one of the most respected black families in Racine. This was Elouise's second marriage. She already had 3 kids: Dianna was 10, Betty was 9, and Wayne was 5. After they were married, Blue and Elouise had 2 more children, Frank and Cheryl. And, Blue had another daughter from an earlier relationship named Mary Anne. She was the same age as Wayne. Life at the Jenkins house was busy!

Elouise: **el** uh weez

79

Many, many nights after work, instead of going home to be with his family, Blue did extra work for the union. He went to meetings, wrote **proposals**, and talked with other union members from the foundry. He and his family made sacrifices so workers could have better lives.

When Blue started out in the union, he had to fight to be recognized. The union was integrated, but even after World War II, Blue was one of just a few black workers at Belle City. He said, "We [the black workers] were never asked to run for union office because we as a group had no **clout**. I vowed that I'd keep running for office in the union until I could be of some use to my people."

Blue knew he could either act like a "sheep" and stay in his place, or he could be "baptized by fire." He chose to be baptized by fire. He would rather push for change and take the heat than stand by and do nothing.

During the early 1950s, Blue fought for services that would help union members. He organized voter **registration** so that

proposal: an offer to do something, often in exchange for something else   **clout** (klout): authority or power
registration: officially signing up

union members would be able to vote in political elections. He started a **blood bank** where union members could **donate** blood and then receive blood if they ever became sick. He set up a program where workers could get **discounts** on medicine and eyeglasses.

As the years passed, people noticed this hardworking leader. Blue earned respect, and people wanted to know what he thought.

Blue, seated in the center, relaxes with fellow union members at a union dinner.

blood bank: a place where blood is stored for when sick people need it   **donate**: give for a good cause
discount: a lower price

During the 1950s, Blue ran for many offices in the union. He joined committees for education and safety, and he eventually became the **chair** of the committees. He worked with the committees for a year or 2 each and then ran for another leadership position. In 1956, he was elected as president of his union, UAW Local 553. He would hold this post for several years.

As a union leader, Blue was very concerned about factory safety. He knew firsthand just how dirty and dangerous foundry work could be. He knew the union had to act and be aware of dangers.

When Blue first worked at Belle City, the factory was dangerous and dirty. Blue said, "When I first went in that foundry, they had **blowers** on the grinders to blow away the metal dust. But they didn't have much suction on them.

chair: the person in charge of a committee   **blower:** a machine that blows air

82

When you'd come out, it would be just like you'd taken black powder and put it on your face. You'd take off your goggles and just see the part where your goggles were, and all the rest of your face would be black. Your lungs would be black. You'd just spit up big **clods** of dirt."

That "dirt" was called **emery dust**. Workers were breathing in tiny pieces of metal and rock from the grinding operation.

"I've had a lung examination," Blue said. "It showed my lungs were really scarred." Some workers had more than scars on their lungs. They got a sickness called **silicosis**. They coughed and struggled to breathe. Sometimes they died.

Breathing dust wasn't the only danger workers faced. Blue saw people badly hurt.

A poster from 1921 reminds workers that not following safety rules has a cost.

clod: a large lump of soil   **emery** (em ree *or* em uh ree) **dust**: dust that comes off a grinder during the grinding of metal   **silicosis** (sil uh **koh** suhs): a lung disease that is caused by breathing in dust. The dust damages the lungs and causes shortness of breath.

"I've seen fellows get their legs broken from a 30-inch wheel," he said. Foundry workers worked with steel and iron. Sometimes a piece of metal would fly into the wheel on a large machine.

Blue said, "Chunks of wheel—big chunks—would hit a guy. Maybe cut off a couple fingers. Break a leg. Put an eye out."

Dangers like these were at the top of the union's list of demands when they met with the Belle City owners to talk about workers' contracts. These contracts were agreements between the union and the factory owners. They included things like how much a union worker was paid to do a certain job and how many hours a day workers needed to work. Contracts also included rules that the company needed to follow to keep workers safe.

When Blue was elected president of the union at Belle City in 1956, he walked through the whole plant every day.

A Chicago factory inspector makes sure a machine has enough oil at the McCormick Twine Mill.

He'd write down every safety problem. He talked to men who had been hurt to find out what had happened. Then Blue talked with company owners.

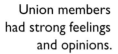

Union members had strong feelings and opinions.

Change came slowly, but little by little, unions demanded and got safer places to work. At some companies, like Belle City, owners realized that they couldn't make money if workers were hurt and sick from dangerous conditions.

By the time Blue retired from factory work in 1968, Belle City was one of the best and cleanest in the whole country.

Blue knew that one answer to safety problems was education. Workers needed education to do their jobs faster and better. Leaders needed education to organize people and solve problems. So Blue got all the education he could.

The University of Wisconsin in Madison had started a
School for Workers. Leaders like Blue came from all over
Wisconsin to learn. The teachers at the School for Workers
were leaders in the union. Blue took classes in political
science. He also became an expert in time study. Time study
means looking carefully at how much time each job takes.
Time-study **experts** figure out better and quicker ways to do
any job. They also pay attention to safe ways to work.

These students are looking at the classes and topics offered at the
University of Wisconsin School for Workers.

expert: someone who knows a lot about a topic

Time Study

Time study is a way companies and workers try to be quicker at making products. A time-study expert watches a worker and uses a stopwatch to find out how long a worker should take to do a particular job quickly but safely. Based on this information, the expert decides how much time a job should take and how much a person should be paid to do it. This makes it easier for both workers and employers to know how well a worker is working.

Time study became popular in the 1920s. Since then, many different methods have been created. At the University of Wisconsin School for Workers, Blue learned how time study worked and how to perform time studies on his own. Using this knowledge, Blue became important as the time-study steward for his union. When the union and the company agreed on rules, it was the steward's job to make sure everyone followed those rules. Blue used time study to make sure workers worked hard and were paid correctly for the amount of work they did.

Blue learned to watch and think. Summer after summer, he went to Madison for a few weeks and studied. Then he returned to Belle City with a head full of information and ideas. Soon the union chose Blue to represent them when problems came up about time study. In 1954, he became the time-study steward for the Belle City union.

Saving time meant saving money. It also meant more pay for workers. At Belle City, workers had to do a certain amount of work every day to get paid. If they worked faster, they were paid extra. This was called **incentive**. If they worked slower, their pay was cut.

The time-study steward's job was to figure out the amount of work that should go into a job and how much a person should be paid for it. Owners always wanted more work. The union tried to make sure men weren't expected to work too fast or too hard. Working too fast causes accidents. Working too fast for too long just wears people out.

Blue was the head time-study man for the union. The Belle City owners had their own time-study person too. Sometimes Blue and the owners' time-study expert would disagree about how much workers should be expected to do or how much a job should pay.

incentive: encouragement to do something

When contracts were signed, the company and union agreed on how a job should be done and how much it should pay. The contract said nobody—not the workers or the owners—could change a job's pay unless the way of doing the job or the object being made was changed.

Then a man named Willy Ed Hardin started to work at Belle City. "This guy was tremendous," Blue said. Willy Ed worked faster than anyone else. "He was strong as a bull. He made 10 dollars an hour." Back in the 1940s and 1950s, 10 dollars an hour was a *lot* of money.

"Willy Ed was making parts for Nash cars," Blue explained. "He'd grind those things up so fast. He was on **snag grinding**. He'd [grind] them and toss them—zip! Other guys had to lay them down and turn them. This guy would toss them in his hand—zip!—and catch them, he [was] so strong."

Soon the bosses realized Willy Ed was making more money than anybody else with the same job. They decided to "cut" the job. They wanted to change the amount of work a snag

snag grinding: finishing a molded piece of metal by grinding off small pieces of it that stick out

grinder was expected to do so they could pay Willy Ed less money. Other snag grinders would be expected to work harder for the same pay.

Blue wasn't happy when he heard the news. "Under our contract, the only way the owners could cut the job was if there had been a change in the **methods** or design."

The boss said to Willy Ed, "You were grinding from right to left. I want you to go from left to right." Of course, that wasn't a change at all!

"But he's doing **identical** work," Blue argued.

Even so, the bosses cut the job. Blue told them the union was stepping in.

The union stood up for Willy Ed. Union men didn't want to strike, but they would strike before they allowed any member to be cheated. *We won't back down*, the union was saying. Finally, the bosses backed down. Willy Ed kept working. And he kept making more money than anybody else.

method: a way of doing something   **identical**: the same

10

Fighting For Equality

By the end of the 1950s, Blue was a leader in both the black community and the union. Black workers and white workers came to him for advice. It was clear that Blue wasn't willing to "stay in his place" like he did in high school. He wasn't willing to be quiet when discrimination happened. Times were changing, and Blue had changed too.

Blue realized that black workers weren't being trained to move up to better jobs in the foundries and other businesses. They were only being trained to do the jobs they already had. Again and again, Blue saw black men **passed over** for promotions.

Seeing discrimination only made Blue work harder for equality. "Some people can't stand **defeat**," he said. "Me, it'd just make me fight harder, because I'm that type of individual."

passed over: when someone isn't even given a chance to try for a better job   **defeat**: being beaten at something

92

Discrimination was still a big problem in the union. Some unions still refused to **admit** black workers. Mr. Oliver, a good friend of Blue's, was a skilled carpenter. He applied for a job with a building company. The owners said they only hired union workers. So Blue's friend went to join the Carpenters' Union.

The Carpenters' Union claimed to be a union for all carpenters. It wasn't true. The Carpenters' Union had a rule

WHI IMAGE ID 6188

White workers in the Carpenters' Union

admit: to allow someone to enter or join

that a member of the union had to **approve** a man's work before he could join the union. Mr. Oliver was an excellent carpenter. But because he was black, no white carpenter would approve his work. So he couldn't join the union.

Mr. Oliver was caught in a game of racism between business owners and unions. Some business owners didn't want to hire black workers. Some unions didn't want black members. So the Carpenters' Union made it impossible for black carpenters to join. That way, business owners could say they weren't discriminating against black workers. *After all*, they'd say, *we agreed to hire only union workers*!

Blue knew this was happening. It made him feel angry. But what could he do about it?

Carpenters, plumbers, and **electricians** were considered "**tradesmen**" —people who worked in the "skilled trades." Often, tradesmen's unions (or "trade unions") discriminated against black workers. Foundry and factory workers like Blue were **fortunate**. They could join **industrial** unions because

approve: to say something is good enough   **electrician**: someone who puts in or fixes electrical wires and equipment   **tradesman**: a worker who does a skilled job   **fortunate** (**for** chuh nit): lucky
industrial (in **dus** tree uhl): having to do with factories

Skilled workers, like these carpenters, often received special training to do their jobs.

they were laborers. But as laborers, they didn't perform jobs that required special training in the factory. Instead, they worked in the foundry, a part of the factory that didn't require "skilled" labor.

Blue had experienced union discrimination in his own family. His dad was a tradesman who couldn't get into a trade union in Racine. Blue remembered, "My dad was quite handy with plastering and bricklaying. He did a lot of plumbing in the South and carpenter work. But when he came up here, he never could get into the unions for that."

Blue's dad finally joined a union in the foundry. But Blue said, "He never could get into the skilled trades."

While the battle for equality was heating up with the skilled trade unions, Blue and his union had fights of their own.

Their union hired a **labor organizer**. This man traveled from city to city, helping unions to plan and to educate and train workers. He taught workers about their rights. He helped natural leaders like Blue learn how to organize their unions and make conditions better for workers.

Leaders like Blue became more and more important in Racine as time went on. Every year, more companies tried to break contracts. More unions voted to strike.

labor organizer: a union expert who gives advice to unions and tries to make them bigger and stronger

96

WHI IMAGE ID 43031

Sometimes part of a strike was refusing to buy anything from the company. The sign on this car says, "We ask you not to buy Wilson products." This was called a **boycott**.

Sometimes strikes lasted months or even years. Sometimes workers and owners both refused to give an inch. Neither side would **compromise**.

Workers would go on strike and refuse to work. Or owners would lock the doors and refuse to let workers come in and do their jobs. Owners had to try to keep their business going. But no union members anywhere would work for them or even help the owners do business. For example, union truck drivers wouldn't pick up or deliver anything to a company where workers were on strike. That's what happened at J. I. Case Company in Racine.

boycott: to refuse to buy something or do business with someone as a protest   **compromise** (**kom** pruh mɪz): agree to accept something that is not exactly what you wanted

Strikers at the J. I. Case strike in 1960. What "points" were the workers fighting for?

Blue said, "Case had some awful strikes. Long ones. **Desperate** ones. Some strikes that tore that union apart."

It was 1960, and Case workers wanted better pay. The owners refused. When workers voted to strike, Case owners

desperate (**des** pur it): almost hopeless

98

decided to destroy the union. This was called "breaking the union."

Day after day, in heat or cold, rain or sun, Case workers marched up and down in front of the company carrying signs. *Unfair to Workers*, the signs said.

The owners hired nonunion "scab" workers. Then the workers formed a solid line of men in front of the doors. They stared and yelled at the scabs. Sometimes they begged scabs not to cross the picket line because the owners were trying to break the union. *Don't help them*, the picketers would beg. *If they break the union, who will protect workers like you?*

Months passed. The owners refused to talk. Striking workers couldn't pay their rent or feed their families. They had trouble coming up with union dues.

Blue and other union leaders were afraid the violence that had happened in other cities might happen in Racine too.

Strike!

Here are some important strikes that happened in Wisconsin:

Year	Who?	What Happened?
1886	Milwaukee workers form a **general strike** and demand an 8-hour workday.	The National Guard, called in by Governor Jeremiah Rusk, opened fire on marching workers in Milwaukee's Bay View neighborhood. Seven people were killed and many more were injured. This became known as the Bay View **Massacre**.
1898	Oshkosh woodworkers strike to get better pay.	Workers were on strike for 14 weeks. Famous lawyer Clarence Darrow defended 3 strikers in court who were charged with **conspiracy**.
1933	Dairy farmers strike for higher milk prices.	The farmers set up road blocks and dumped the milk of some larger milk producers who tried to keep selling.
1934	Kohler Company workers strike for better pay, shorter hours, and a new union.	On the night of July 27, protesters and others from nearby towns fought with police and company guards. Two men were killed and 47 others were injured.

general strike: a strike by workers at many companies and different jobs, not just at one factory or company
massacre (**mass** uh ker): a cruel act of killing of innocent people   **conspiracy** (kuhn **spir** uh see): secretly planning to do something illegal or dangerous

During the milk strike, workers dumped hundreds of gallons of milk in protest.

A poster supporting the Kohler strike

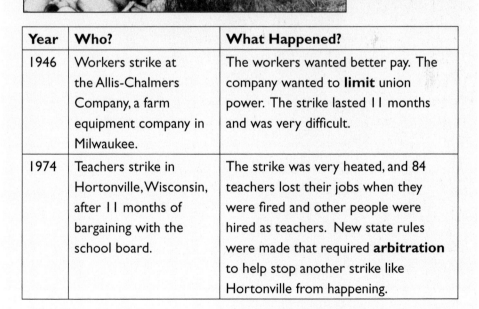

Year	Who?	What Happened?
1946	Workers strike at the Allis-Chalmers Company, a farm equipment company in Milwaukee.	The workers wanted better pay. The company wanted to **limit** union power. The strike lasted 11 months and was very difficult.
1974	Teachers strike in Hortonville, Wisconsin, after 11 months of bargaining with the school board.	The strike was very heated, and 84 teachers lost their jobs when they were fired and other people were hired as teachers. New state rules were made that required **arbitration** to help stop another strike like Hortonville from happening.

limit: to hold back and not let go any farther   **arbitration** (ahr buh **tray** shuhn): having someone such as a lawyer come in to help 2 sides reach a fair agreement

The Case strike dragged on. During the long strike, workers had no **income**. Their families were suffering. Some men wanted to give up. Others said no. The union was falling apart. Blue and other union men had to help.

Blue joined the Case workers at the picket line. "After I'd get off from work, I'd walk the picket line with them. Then we heard that the owners were going to try to pull a load of tractors out of there with the trains."

Sometimes kids joined the picket lines!

income: wages

During many strikes, like this one in 1962 in Milwaukee, blacks and whites stood together.

The Case owners had hired enough scab workers to build some tractors. Now they were trying to ship the tractors to stores. If they managed to make a profit using scab workers, there would be no need to hire union workers back. The tractor shipment needed to be stopped.

News spread that the strikers were in trouble. Union workers all over Racine left their jobs in the middle of the day and rushed to the Case Company.

At Case, scab workers were loading shiny new tractors onto train cars. Strikers stood around, angry and frustrated. They were so **discouraged**. They'd marched and carried picket signs for months. They'd tried and tried to get the owners to listen. They'd risked their jobs and lost months of pay in hopes of getting a better contract. Now everything seemed lost.

Blue and some other union men arrived. They shook hands and stood with the strikers. Then one of them walked to the train tracks. He sat down right in front of the train engine. Then another sat next to him. Then another. Then Blue.

Soon the tracks were filled with sitting men. The trains couldn't move. If talk and picket signs couldn't get the owners to listen, maybe this would.

discouraged: saddened

Agreements between union workers and factory bosses required listening and patience.

After many months, the Case union and owners finally agreed to a contract. But the long strike had hurt the union. The owners were still determined to break the union. There would be many more strikes at Case before the union became strong again.

11

The Civil Rights Movement
Comes to Racine

On a December evening in 1955, a young woman boarded a city bus in Montgomery, Alabama. Her name was Rosa Parks.

Rosa Parks paid her fare and took a nearby seat. The bus pulled away from the curb. At the next stop, more riders got on. Then more. Soon all the seats in the front of the bus were taken.

Rosa Parks in 1960

The bus driver turned to Rosa Parks. He demanded that she get up and give her seat to another rider. A white rider.

At the bus station in Durham, North Carolina, there were separate waiting rooms for blacks and whites.

She shook her head. No. She had paid her fare just like everyone else. She refused to stand just because she was black. She wouldn't give her seat to a white person.

Many hundreds of miles north, in Racine, Wisconsin, Blue Jenkins heard how Rosa Parks had refused to give her seat on a bus to a white passenger. He read the newspaper and listened to television news reports. Rosa Parks's decision grew into a movement that spread across the entire United States. It came to be called the Civil Rights Movement. And soon, Blue became part of it.

While people were marching for equal rights in Mississippi and black citizens were refusing to ride any bus in Montgomery, Alabama, Blue Jenkins was working for civil rights here in Wisconsin.

Starting in the 1950s, Blue had been involved with

the NAACP, the National **Association** for the **Advancement** of Colored People. The NAACP had members in every state fighting for racial equality. Blue's father-in-law, George Bray, was the first leader of the NAACP in Racine. When he retired in 1956, Blue took over as president.

Blue when he joined the NAACP

association (uh soh see **ay** shuhn): a group of people joined together for a common reason   **advancement**: progress or moving forward

108

One of the first things Blue did as president was to get his local union involved. Why would the union want to take part? After all, it was integrated, with both white members and black members. What did the union have to do with civil rights?

Quite a lot, in fact.

In Racine, when union members at one company went on strike, union members from other companies stood by them. In the same way, union members stood up for the rights of African Americans. Blue convinced Local 553 to join the NAACP. He even collected

This union worker is protesting against racial discrimination outside a Woolworth store. What does his sign say?

At this labor rally, people carried signs to fight discrimination.

money from the union to help support the protests and **sit-ins** that were taking place in the South during the years after Rosa Parks's bus ride.

Like Blue, Martin Luther King Jr. believed civil rights were closely linked to workers' rights. He visited striking workers in Memphis, Tennessee, in 1968 and spoke these words: "Our struggle is for **genuine** equality, which means economic

sit-in: a protest in which people sit in seats or on the floor at a business that uses discrimination
genuine (jen yoo uhn): real and not fake

110

equality. For now we know that it isn't enough to integrate lunch counters. What does it **profit** a man to be able to eat at an integrated lunch counter if he doesn't earn enough money to buy a hamburger and a cup of coffee?"

Martin Luther King Jr. with union leaders. King is in the center.

Blue and others like him fought for the "economic equality" King talked about. They believed it applied to all people, in the North and in the South, black or white, union member or everyday citizen.

And in unions, treatment of all workers became important, and blacks and whites stood together to fight for their rights.

profit: benefit or help

Even though great gains were made in the 1960s, discrimination was part of daily life for every black person in Racine. Blue knew which stores wouldn't hire black workers. He knew which taverns he could enter and be welcome and where he'd be glared at by angry white customers. He also knew which neighborhoods he could buy a house in and which he couldn't.

Even in 1965, blacks were told where they could and couldn't live.

Blue and Elouise had worked and saved to buy a cozy house for their family. They wanted to live on a nice, clean street with friendly neighbors. On Sunday afternoons, they'd drive around Racine checking out houses with For Sale signs on their front lawns.

But the Jenkins family wasn't welcome in every neighborhood. Blue earned a good income at the foundry. They could afford to buy a house. But the problem was finding an owner willing to sell to them and a bank willing to give them a loan.

Blue told what happened. "I was trying to buy a house here in Racine. I'd go to the house and as soon as they saw I was black, they turned me down. In fact, I got to the point where I let my wife and mother-in-law go to these places. My mother-in-law was fair. And my wife, you can't tell her from white if you didn't know.

"So, I let them go to the house, talk about the house, and go through it. I would park a block away and then pick them up. I said, 'If you like it, we'll buy it.' We'd put down **earnest money**.

"They'd find out we were black and they'd up the price on us, or something would happen so we couldn't buy the house. I was getting pretty frustrated."

earnest (**ur** nist) **money**: money put down as a promise to buy something

Black families everywhere in the United States had the same experience. Home owners refused to sell their houses to black buyers. Or banks would only lend money to black families if the houses they were buying were in the "black" neighborhoods. Even men like Blue, with well-paying jobs in the foundries, were turned down for loans whenever the house they wanted to buy was in a "white" neighborhood.

One of Blue's white friends, **Eddy Shamshoian**, was furious when he heard how Blue was being treated. "I tell you what," Eddy said. "We'll buy the house and we'll turn it over to you. You pick one out."

Eddy Shamshoian knew his white neighbors would be very angry if he sold a house to any black family. But he didn't care.

Blue and Eloise said no to their friend's kind offer. They didn't want to live where their neighbors disliked them. They didn't want Eddy's family to have trouble either.

Eddy Shamshoian: ed ee sham **shoh** yuhn

During the 1950s, '60s, and '70s, Blue Jenkins worked for civil rights. He encouraged other men to take a stand in their community. But at times the fight for equal rights could get ugly.

In 1967, a local pastor organized a big group of kids to march for civil rights in Racine. A **riot** happened. White people yelled at the marchers. Someone yelled a hateful word at the **protestors**. A rock was thrown in response.

WHI IMAGE ID 59547

Some civil rights protests got violent, like this one in Milwaukee in 1965.

riot (**rī** uht): a violent and disordered group of people   **protestor**: someone who objects to something in public

115

People began pushing and shoving. Then fights started everywhere. People got hurt, and the mayor actually shut down the whole city for a day.

Father Groppi, a priest from Milwaukee, led demonstrations against school segregation.

Blue was very concerned that the pastor had young kids marching. He said kids shouldn't be where violence could happen. "It's not a kids' fight," he said. "It's the young adults' and adults' fight."

Blue began to talk to anybody who would listen. He knew people had been killed during civil rights protests in other cities. In Detroit and Chicago, there were violent riots. Blue didn't want that to happen in Racine. He used every tool he'd learned during his years with the union. He argued. He reasoned. He ignored hurtful words and tried to make peace. He calmed angry people. But he didn't back down.

12

Last Years in the Union

In 1962, Blue ran for the most important office in his union—and won. Suddenly, he was in charge of all of the union foundry workers in the Midwest. Imagine. When he started at Belle City, no one saw him as a leader. Now he was working for the rights of 50,000 people!

Blue took on other leadership roles too. In 1962, the same year he became president of the Midwest foundry workers, he was also in charge of **grievances** for his local union. A grievance happened when a union member made a complaint. Perhaps the contract wasn't being followed, or a worker wasn't being treated fairly. It was Blue's job to **investigate** and report back to the union. Then the union would send a letter to put pressure on the factory owners to change things.

grievance (**gree** vuhns): a formal complaint or objection   **investigate**: to find out as much as possible about something

As grievance chairman, Blue had the chance to strike a strong blow against discrimination. This chance wasn't in Racine, but miles away in Janesville.

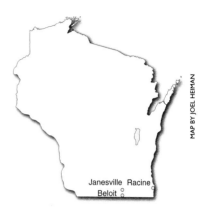

MAP BY JOEL HEIMAN

Janesville Racine
Beloit

Blue knew discrimination was a problem in Janesville. In Janesville, only white workers were hired. In fact, not a single black worker was hired at Janesville's Chevrolet auto plant. And Blue's union, the United Auto Workers, wanted to know why.

At that time, every local union in the United Auto Workers was supposed to make sure workers weren't turned down for jobs because of race. But in Janesville, the local union didn't say a word. So the state union directors sent Blue to find out what was really happening.

"Back then Janesville was the most **peculiar** town," Blue said. "As a black person, you could do anything you wanted in that town but live and get a job. You could start a business of your own, but you couldn't live there."

peculiar (pi **kyool** yur): strange

118

This organization shall be known as the INTERNATIONAL FOUNDRY WAGE AND HOUR COUNCIL of the U. A. W.

ARTICLE 2

Objects

Section 1. The purpose of this organization is to better acquaint the Foundry Workers with conditions of the different Foundries.

Section 2. To take wages out of competition by establishing a standard wage for all the Foundry Workers.

Section 3. To eliminate discrimination on account of race, color or creed.

Section 4. To unite as many Foundries as possible to strengthen our fight for better wages, working conditions and shorter hours.

Section 5. To educate Foundry Workers of their legal rights provided by the existing laws.

Section 6. To help organize all unorganized and competitive Foundries into the UAW.

Section 7. To gather data concerning wages, hours and working conditions for the purpose of providing a constant flow of information to all Sub-Councils.

Blue helped write this list of goals, or "objects," for the UAW International Foundry Union. Which goal was the Janesville plant not following?

Blue met a black restaurant owner from Janesville. "This guy had a beautiful restaurant. White customers crowded it every night." But because of discrimination, that man couldn't live where he owned a business. Instead, he lived in Beloit, about 15 miles south.

"The union sent a fellow by the name of Ross from Detroit in with me," Blue explained. "I was doing most of the investigating. And I found out they had what they called 'The Ring' there in Janesville. The Ring consisted of the newspaper, the church, somebody from Parker Pen Company, and one black man by the name of Davis."

Blue found out that the men in The Ring had power to decide who would and who wouldn't get jobs in Janesville. Blue and Ross talked to black and white people all over town. Quickly, it became clear to Blue and Ross that the Chevrolet plant and other businesses weren't hiring black workers in Janesville because the men in the "ring" wanted to keep those high-paying jobs for white workers.

Davis, the black man in The Ring, was part of the conspiracy. His family was the only black family in Janesville, and he wanted to protect his place in the community.

Blue and Ross told the Fair Employment Practices Division of the union why black workers weren't being hired at the Chevrolet plant in Janesville. Nothing changed right away, but Blue and Ross's report was like a spark. That spark would light a fire that, in time, would bring change.

Although Blue enjoyed being a leader, he learned that he preferred to work on a more local level with men he knew, rather than in a top position. Those at the top tended to lose sight of those at the bottom. Blue said, "The leaders stay in there so long, they forget what it is to be in the plant again. They get **status** crazy, and they don't give you the protection you should really have."

Blue wasn't interested in power. He was interested in helping workers claim their rights. Instead of running again for president of the Midwest foundry union, he chose to step down at the end of his term.

A few years later, in 1968, Blue retired from Belle City Malleable. But he didn't stop working. Although he left the union behind, he kept working for workers.

Blue became the manager of R.E.C. Industries. R.E.C. was a free program for young men who were out of work. These

status (**stat** uhs): a person's position or rank

Blue helps a young man think about his career goals.

men lacked the experience that would get them good jobs in Racine's factories. At R.E.C., they were trained to be skilled factory workers. They became experts on many factory machines. Local companies like J. I. Case donated machines, tools, **instructors**, and space.

R.E.C. taught the men more than job skills. Blue said, "The program is changing the basic attitudes of the **trainees**; there

instructor: teacher   trainee (tray nee): someone being trained

are blacks, Mexicans, and whites here, and they're learning to work together to gain skills."

Thirty years before, Blue faced a great amount of discrimination in his workplace. Now young men from every kind of background were working together to get to the factory floor.

Young men learning new skills at R.E.C. Industries

13

A Life Well Lived

Until the end of his life, Blue continued to be a leader in the community. Black and white people came to Blue for advice. They trusted him and respected his ideas.

In time, people in the black community in Racine began to call Blue the "Mayor of **Bronzeville**." (Bronzeville was an area in Chicago where a lot of African Americans lived.) Being called Mayor of Bronzeville was an honor. It has nothing to do with votes or elections. It

Blue called Elouise his "queen."

Bronzeville: bronz vil

meant people recognized that Blue was one of the most important leaders in the community.

Blue and Elouise Jenkins lived the rest of their lives in Racine. They raised a large family. They bought a cozy house— and even had some friendly white neighbors. Often, relatives' children lived with them. Blue encouraged and supported his children to go to college. His stepson, Wayne, became a college professor. His nephew, Gooch Jenkins,

Blue's wife, Elouise (second from the left), poses with their children Betty, Frank, Dianna, and Cheryl.

Blue with his grandson Marcus

played football for the University of Wisconsin and started programs all over the state to keep people off drugs.

After Blue retired, he stayed active in his community. He spent his time **volunteering** and taking care of his grandkids.

Blue called Racine a "unique place." He was right. Racine was unique in some ways. But in other ways, Racine was like many towns and cities in Wisconsin and across the United States. And Blue's life in Racine was a **snapshot** of the lives of many black people in America.

During Blue's 84 years of life, he saw changes in attitudes and ideas. His own children went to college. No one told them to stay in their place.

Blue knew racism was still in the hearts and actions of some people. He knew that discrimination still existed in some workplaces. But he believed most people wanted equality. And he believed most people were willing to work for the good of everyone.

volunteering: offering to do something without getting paid for it   **snapshot**: an informal picture or example

Appendix

Blue Jenkins's Time Line

1916 — On April 16, William "Blue" Jenkins is born in Hattiesburg, Mississippi, to Frank and Irene (Lindsey) Jenkins. Six months later, Blue and his parents move to Racine, Wisconsin.

1929 — Blue gets his driver's license.

1936 — In January, Blue graduates from Horlick High School in Racine.

1938 — Blue begins working at Belle City Malleable in Racine.

1941 — Blue becomes chairman of Fair Employment Practices Committee, UAW Local 553.

1944–1948 — Blue serves as chairman of several committees for Local 553, including recreation, education, and political action.

1949 — Blue begins taking summer classes at the School for Workers.

1950 — Blue marries Elouise Bray.

1954 — Blue serves as chief time-study steward, Local 553.

1956 — Blue becomes president of UAW-CIO Local 553 and of the NAACP in Racine.

1962 — Blue becomes president of the UAW National Foundry Sub-council No. 2; serves as chairman of the Bargaining and Grievance Committee, Local 553; and serves on the Mayor's Commission on Human Rights in Racine.

1963 — Blue serves as member of Steering Committee for the Racine Urban League.

1964–1966 — Blue serves as President of Central Labor Council, AFL-CIO, in Racine.

1965 — Blue takes part in an antiracism rally in Racine.

1966 — Blue becomes cochairman of the Labor Committee for the Racine United Fund and begins volunteering with Big Brothers of Racine.

1968 — Blue retires from Belle City Malleable (Racine Steel Castings) after 30 years. He becomes manager of R.E.C. Industries, Inc.

1972 — Blue retires.

1999 — Blue dies of heart failure on April 6 in Racine.

Glossary

Pronunciation Key

a   cat (kat), plaid (plad), half (haf)

ah   father (**fah** THur), heart (hahrt)

air   carry (**kair** ee), bear (bair), where (whair)

aw   all (awl), law (law), bought (bawt)

ay   say (say), break (brayk), vein (vayn)

e   bet (bet), says (sez), deaf (def)

ee   bee (bee), team (teem), fear (feer)

i   bit (bit), women (**wim** uhn), build (bild)

ɪ   ice (ɪs), lie (lɪ), sky (skɪ)

o   hot (hot), watch (wotch)

oh   open (**oh** puhn), sew (soh)

oi   boil (boil), boy (boi)

oo   pool (pool), move (moov), shoe (shoo)

or   order (**or** dur), more (mor)

ou   house (hous), now (nou)

u   good (gud), should (shud)

uh   cup (kuhp), flood (fluhd), button (**buht** uhn)

ur   burn (burn), pearl (purl), bird (burd)

yoo   use (yooz), few (fyoo), view (vyoo)

hw   what (hwuht), when (hwen)

TH   that (THat), breathe (breeTH)

zh   measure (**mezh** ur), garage (guh **razh**)

129

ace: very good

admit: to allow someone to enter or join

advancement: progress or moving forward

affected: changed or influenced

ally (**al** ī): friend, especially during a war

application: a written request

approve: to say something is good enough

arbitration (ahr buh **tray** shuhn): having someone such as a lawyer come in to help 2 sides reach a fair agreement

assemble: put together

association (uh soh see **ay** shuhn): a group of people joined together for a common reason

automotive industry: the companies that make cars and other vehicles

banding: forming a group to achieve a common purpose

benefit: a special advantage that comes with a job such as time off when you're sick

big time: the top level, as in the Major League

blew my top: got really angry

blood bank: a place where blood is stored for when sick people need it

blower: a machine that blows air

blue collar: working with your hands instead of in an office or store

bomber: a plane whose main job is to drop bombs on targets

bootlegger: someone who makes or sells alcohol illegally

boycott: to refuse to buy something or do business with someone as a protest

brakeman: a train worker who operates the train's brakes

cast iron: iron mixed with other metals to form a very hard metal

cattle cars: trailers used for shipping animals from one place to another

chair: the person in charge of a committee

chancellor (**chan** suh lur): the leader of a country, similar to a president

chest protector: a pad worn to shield a catcher's chest

Civil Rights Movement: the movement from the mid-1950s through the 1960s for African Americans to have fair and equal treatment under the law

Civil War: the war between the North and South of the United States, which took place between 1861 and 1865

clod: a large lump of soil

clout (klout): authority or power

collective bargaining rights: the right of employees to come to an agreement with their employer about wages, hours, and other things

committee (kuh **mit** ee): a group of people chosen to go over a topic and make a decision

compromise (**kom** pruh mɪz): agree to accept something that is not exactly what you wanted

conductor: a train worker who collects tickets and keeps the train on schedule

conquer (**kong** kur): beat and become master of

conspiracy (kuhn **spir** uh see): secretly planning to do something illegal or dangerous

contract: an agreement between a worker and an employer about pay and other issues

core room: a room of a foundry where the molds used to shape metal are made

defeat: being beaten at something

demand: an official request

desperate (**des** pur it): almost hopeless

discount: a lower price

discouraged: saddened

discrimination: unfair treatment of people, based on differences such as race, age, or place of birth

donate: give for a good cause

dropped out: quit going to school

dues: money paid to an organization, such as a union, to help it run

earnest (**ur** nist) **money**: money put down as a promise to buy something

electrician: someone who puts in or fixes electrical wires and equipment

emery (**em** ree *or* **em** uh ree) **dust**: dust that comes off a grinder during the grinding of metal

equipment: tools needed for a particular purpose

expert: someone who knows a lot about a topic

fair: having light-colored skin or hair

fortunate (**for** chuh nit): lucky

foundry (**foun** dree): a factory where metal is melted and shaped

fraternity: a feeling of equality among people

gambler: someone who bets money on a game, race, or other contest

general strike: a strike by workers at many companies and different jobs, not just at one factory or company

genuine (**jen** yoo uhn): real and not fake

Great Depression: the decade of the 1930s when many people in the United States had no jobs and were very poor

grievance (**gree** vuhns): a formal complaint or objection

identical: the same

immigrant (**im** uh gruhnt): someone who leaves a country to permanently live in another country

incentive: encouragement to do something

income: wages

industrial (in **dus** tree uhl): having to do with factories

instigator (**in** stuh gay tur): the person who starts something

instructor: teacher

integrated: made to include people of all races

interest: the cost for borrowing money, usually based on the amount borrowed

investigate: to find out as much as possible about something

janitor: someone who takes care of and cleans a building

job interview: a meeting to see if someone should be hired for a job

junkyard: a place that collects and resells old stuff no one wants, such as wrecked cars

Ku Klux Klan: a racist group that believes whites are better than other races

laborer: someone who works with their hands doing physical labor

labor organizer: a union expert who gives advice to unions and tries to make them bigger and stronger

labor union (**yoo** nyuhn): an organization of workers set up to improve things such as working conditions, health benefits, and the amount people are paid to work

laid off: let go from a job because there isn't enough work to do or enough money to pay workers

laying track: building train tracks

license: an official card that says a person is allowed to drive

lick: beat

limit: to hold back and not let go any farther

live: in person at a concert, not recorded

maintenance (**mayn** tuh nuhns): fixing or maintaining machines or buildings

malleable (**mal** ee uh buhl): soft and easy to shape

manager: a person in charge of a business or other employees at work

massacre (**mass** uh ker): a cruel act of killing of innocent people

method: a way of doing something

migration (mɪ **gray** shuhn): movement from one community to another in the same country

minority: someone of a small race or ethnic group that lives among a larger race or ethnic group

negro: a name people used in the past for African Americans. People now think the word is disrespectful.

office: a leadership job

on strike: refusing to go to work until an employer agrees to change something

organized: arranged in order to work together

outgoing: warm, friendly, and confident

outraged: very angry

passed over: when someone isn't even given a chance to try for a better job

pavilion: a building with open sides used for outdoor music and dancing

peculiar (pi **kyool** yur): strange

picket sign: a sign carried by a protester during a strike

porter: a train worker who handles luggage

professional sports: sports played at a high level and where the players are paid to play

profit: benefit or help

Prohibition (proh uh **bish** uhn): the period between 1920 and 1933 in which it was illegal to make or sell alcohol

promoted: moved to a higher rank or job

propellers: spinning blades that move an airplane through the air or a boat through the water

proposal: an offer to do something, often in exchange for something else

protesting: gathering in public to fight for a cause

protestor: someone who objects to something in public

recruited: encouraged to work for a company

registration: officially signing up

remarkable: worth noticing

riot (**rı** uht): a violent and disordered group of people

rumor: talk or an opinion that people tell each other, passing it on without knowing if it is true or not

scab: a worker who takes the job of someone on strike

scholarship (**skah** ler ship): money given to help a student continue studying

seed money: money borrowed to buy seeds or start a new business

semi-professional: playing for money, but not all the time

separate but equal: the idea that blacks and whites could be made to use different restaurants, stores, schools, and other things, as long as the places and things were equally good

shabby: dirty and poorly made

sharecropper: a poor farmer who has no money to rent land to farm. To pay the rent, sharecroppers give the landowner a "share" of their crops.

shell: a small bomb that is fired from a cannon or tank

signed on: agreed to work for

silicosis (sil uh **koh** suhs): a lung disease that is caused by breathing in dust. The dust damages the lungs and causes shortness of breath.

single: not married

sit-down strike: a strike where workers refuse to work and just sit down on the job instead

sit-in: a protest in which people sit in seats or on the floor at a business that uses discrimination

skilled job: a job that requires special training and usually pays well

snag grinding: finishing a molded piece of metal by grinding off small pieces of it that stick out

snapshot: an informal picture or example

social club: a place similar to a restaurant or a bar where people meet to have fun

soda fountain: a place where you can buy soda drinks, often with ice cream in them

sponsored: gave money and support to, usually in return for some advertising

status (**stat** uhs): a person's position or rank

steward (**stoo** urd): a union member who works with the company to make sure both the company and the union are following their contract

swing dancing: energetic dancing done to band music that was popular in the 1930s

swing grinder: a worker who uses a grinding machine that hangs from a chain

swingingest: a slang word for most fun or exciting

tradesman: a worker who does a skilled job

trainee (tray **nee**): someone being trained

tuition: money paid to take classes

unit: a military group of small size

vacation pay: pay for workers on days they don't come in to work but instead go on vacation

varsity letter: a cloth letter given as an award to high school students for doing well in sports or other activities

vocational school: a school where students learn specific skills that help them get jobs as laborers

volunteering: offering to do something without getting paid for it

wage: the money someone is paid to work

white collar: working at an office or store and not doing physical labor

zoot suit: a special suit with a long jacket, big shoulders, and baggy pants

Reading Group Guide and Activities

Discussion Questions

❧ Blue and his family moved to Racine, Wisconsin, for a better life in 1916. Do you think they found a better life? Why or why not? What was good about the life they lived in Racine? What could have been better?

❧ Name three examples in the book where Blue faced discrimination. How did Blue react in each of these cases? How did he work to overcome discrimination? Did he always fight back? Why or why not? What would you do in his place?

❧ When Blue was finished with high school, he had a choice about whether to go to college or stay in Racine. What did he decide, and why? Would you make the same choice, or a different one?

❧ Blue grew up being told to "stay in his place." How did his attitude about staying in his place change after he became part of the union? Why do you think his attitude changed?

❧ Blue fought for both workers' rights and civil rights. What do these two kinds of rights have in common? Why did Blue fight for both?

Activities

We know about Blue's story because a worker from the Wisconsin Historical Society took time to interview him. Choose an older person who has lived in your community for most of his or her life to interview. (You could also interview someone who has taken part in the Civil Rights Movement or someone who is active in a union.) Write down a list of questions to ask the person ahead of time. Bring a digital recorder to record the interview. When the interview is over, prepare a five minute presentation for your class to introduce your interview subject.

As a class, brainstorm a list of issues where something is going on that isn't fair. Examples might include endangered species, pollution, human rights, poverty, or continuing racism. From that list, choose one issue to research further. Find out how that issue affects the city or town where you live. Write a letter to your local representative to ask them to make changes that will make the situation better.

To Learn More about Blue Jenkins, Workers' Rights, and Civil Rights

Brexel, Bernadette. *The Knights of Labor and the Haymarket Riot: The Fight for an Eight-Hour Workday*. New York: Rosen, 2003.

Levine, Ellen S. *Freedom's Children: Young Civil Rights Activists Tell Their Own Stories*. New York: Puffin, 1993.

McNeese, Tim. *The Labor Movement: Unionizing America*. New York: Chelsea House, 2007.

McWhorter, Diane. *A Dream of Freedom: The Civil Rights Movement from 1954 to 1968*. New York: Scholastic Nonfiction, 2004.

Reef, Catherine. *A. Philip Randolph: Union Leader and Civil Rights Crusader*. Berkeley Heights, NJ: Enslow, 2001.

Skurzinsky, Gloria. *Sweat and Blood: A History of U.S. Labor Unions*. Minneapolis: Twenty-First Century Books, 2009.

Stein, R. Conrad. *The Pullman Strike and the Labor Movement in American History*. Berkeley Heights, NJ: Enslow, 2001.

Stokes, John A., with Lois Wolfe. *Students on Strike: Jim Crow, Civil Rights, Brown, and Me*. Washington, DC: National Geographic Children's Books, 2007.

Turck, Mary C. *The Civil Rights Movement for Kids: A History with 21 Activities*. Chicago: Chicago Review Press, 2000.

Acknowledgments

Appreciation goes to Ms. Betty Thomas and "Gooch" and Rose Jenkins for sharing personal stories about Blue and Elouise Jenkins. Many of the family photographs in the final chapters came from Betty. Thanks also to William Horlick High School for photos and facts about Blue's years as a Horlick football star.

The staff of the Wisconsin Historical Society Press deserve applause and appreciation for finding the many interesting photos and illustrations in this book and for contributing valuable details to Blue's story. These include Director of School Services Bobbie Malone, developmental editor Sara Phillips, production editor Diane Drexler, image researcher John Nondorf, and editorial assistants Mallory Kirby, Kate Carey, Carly Wieman, and Rachel Cordasco. Thank you also to the late George Roeder who interviewed Blue Jenkins for the Historical Society, and to the Archives staff for preserving the interviews that made this book possible.

Finally, thanks to John "Jack" Holzhueter who first introduced me to the story of Blue Jenkins and said, "Somebody should write a book about Blue."

Index

This index points you to the pages where you can read about persons, places, and ideas. If you do not find the word you are looking for, try to think of another word that means about the same thing.

When you see a page number in **bold** it means there is a picture on that page.